The Real - Life Woman at the Well

Carol Davis – Doswell

Sivad Publishing
www.tamathaadavis.com
Printed in USA by Ingram Spark
First Edition, November 2024

Cover art (drawing) by Gary Sperling

The Real - Life Woman at the Well

Carol Davis-Doswell

Preface

It happened when my publisher, Tamatha Davis, called me - unexpectedly, and wished me Happy Birthday after many, many years ! Two days later I called her back and asked her if she ever published the book she said she wanted to do.

I never really thought that I had a book in me. I just thought that when the Lord told me to write down all that I had been through over the years, I assumed it was to heal me from the inside. I thought it was so I could move forward with my life.

Additionally, I had no idea where all the writings from years before were located. We had moved so much; I had no idea if I still had them. That was when I took it to the Lord in prayer, *"If you want me to write a book, show me where the papers are"*. Several nights later GOD gave me a dream and showed me right where they were!

I am not one to doubt that the dream was not real! If the Lord said it was in a certain place - "I believed him". However, I did not jump up and go check either! Several days later I was sitting in my art room doing my nails when suddenly I heard the Lord say, *"You are only 10 feet away"*. So, I got up and walked over to a dresser in the hallway, opened the drawer, and there they all were neatly stacked, as though they were just placed there.

I smiled big and knew the reason I had sat down years ago and poured out all my hurt and pain on my computer for several months. The Lord planned for me to write down all my failed marriages so someday it would be a book to help others.

Dedication

I would like to dedicate this book to the *man God made for me –* my husband, Benjamin Louis Doswell. He has always encouraged me to write my story to help other women. I pray it helps them to find Jesus.

Table of Contents

Introduction

This is not just a good story – it's my life from age 17 to 43. You know how the saying goes, *'you have to learn some things the hard way,'* and for the most part, which is true because no one else can walk in your shoes but you! Due to my stubbornness and trust in the world, I chose to do things my way.

If you see yourself in my story, rest assured you are not alone. Know that your story will help others as well. The idea alone of being married more times than I could have ever thought is almost too much to take.

Enter my world, and just maybe you will see yourself.

If it had not been for the Lord, I would not be writing this story. Testimonies are given to the ones who can hold their heads up high and teach others from their experiences. My testimony began in the year 1973 when I was 22 years old, a divorced mother of a son who was then four years old. I wanted so much for someone to love me and be faithful to me. I was not in my nature to cheat nor was it in me to stay with someone who was a cheater. I am getting ahead of myself, so let me tell you truly how it all began.

Before the Well

The Real-Life Woman at the Well

I grew up in a small town in north Texas from the third grade to the twelfth grade. There was something about the innocence of a small town and small-town ways, but we must grow up at some point. My favorite past time was sports-all sports! There was not one at which I was not good.

In my small town, there was a strange, but fun past time. It was called, *"making the drag."* That was when teens with cars full of other teens drove from one end of our small town to the other. It was all of a two-mile round trip. Yes, we considered that to be entertainment in our little town, especially on the weekends.

One night a new guy showed up in a shiny, black '57 Chevy, and it was cool. His name was '*David*'. That was not his real name, as the names have been changed to protect the guilty. He asked several of us girls to hop in his car and, *"make the drag"*. He wanted me to sit next to him in the front and the other girls just piled in. And off we went!

It was not long before *David* came to my house to pick me up to go riding around. At some point he said to me, *"I'd like for you to meet my parents."*

I told him that I would check with my parents to see if it would be okay.

He said, *"It's just about three miles away and I promise we won't stay long."*

I said, *"Okay, but let's hurry."*

This was 1969, so there were no cell phones back then. We drove to the small town he grew up in that was out in the country.

Finally, we drove down a long dirt driveway to a small white house. As we approached the house, *David* honked the horn to let them know we were there. He parked the car in the front yard, and we got out and went inside.

He said aloud, *"We're here!"* but no one answered.

I walked in and the television was on extremely loud! That was when he slammed the front door and locked it. Then he approached me and threw me on the sofa. He began to take off everything! He told me to do the same or he would rip my clothes off.

I screamed, I cried, and I tried to get up, but he over-powered me. I had never heard the words date rape until I got much older, but that is exactly what happened to me.

I think that many of us older women today do not want to talk about what happened to us when we were young. I have always thought that if we expose the enemy for who he is, then we could help teach others to not get caught up in these situations.

In today's world we are seeing children being taken and turned into sex slaves. Yes, we need to talk about our lives and help others through theirs. No matter when it happened to us, women and children need to know we care and are there for them, as we should be.

So, he drove me home. He just dropped me off at my house after he did this to me. We said nothing to each other all the way back to my house. No, apology - nothing. I went straight to the bathroom when I walked in the front door and wiped the blood off from between my legs. I held back the tears and went to bed. The next morning, I told my mom I was not feeling well, and that my tummy hurt. She let me go back to bed. When she came to check on me, she noticed I was crying. I just told her that my tummy hurt. She was very understanding and let me rest.

I hurt so badly, but I was afraid to say anything to my parents. I was not sure how to say anything. My mom and dad were both former Marines and fought in World War II. It would not have been pretty if I had told them what really happened but, looking back, I should have said something, instead of carrying this burden alone.

To say the least, I did not see *David* for a month or so after the rape. When I did see him, he was flirting with other girls. I just did my best to stay away from him. I was just sixteen, about to turn seventeen.

I was, however, a licensed hairstylist along with waiting to be told whether I was accepted at one or two different colleges in the north Texas area at that time. I was training for the junior Olympics in track and field in low hurdles. Plus, I had just earned the number one position in women's singles tennis on our high school tennis team. I had so much going for me. I was about to graduate high school and leave home.

Husband #1:

Nightmare on Nowhere Street

One day at work, doing hair, I realized I had missed my period. I called my dad and said, *"Dad, I do not feel good. Can you come get me and take me home?"*

I told him the story of what had happened to me. From that moment, he pretty much said, *"You made your bed, you lay in it!"*

What he meant was, *"You are going to marry him and have that baby or get an abortion, and I want you out of our house"*

It did not sound fair because what happened was not my fault, but my parents *(mostly my dad)* did not want to hear any excuses. They did not realize the pain I went through being raped, and at this point I was just shocked. I told them that *David* did not know, so they called a lady who was a nurse to find out the details about an abortion.

I told them *"No, I'm not going to do that!"*

It was the last thing on my mind to do, so I got ahold of *David* and asked him to come over for dinner. I think he was glad I asked him. So here I am, a month and a half pregnant when my dad broke the news and told him that the two of us needed to get married or he was going to see that he went to jail for rape!

My mom was horrified that my dad made that decision, but back in 1969 that was the way things were. The Beatles were #1 on the music charts. Jimmy Hendricks was famous. Woodstock was happening and I was pregnant and afraid of the guy I was about to marry.

My parents did not know what was going on until my mom came to see me one day while he was at work. My mom had no idea I was being so mistreated and abused. I was due in just a few months, and by then I wished I were dead!

The Real- Life Woman at the Well

I lived in the same house where I was raped, so the memory was in my face constantly. Just to give you an idea of my living conditions. I had no phone to call anyone for help. There were snakes and rats the size of a cat that could get into the house through all sorts of cracks and holes. There was no tv or radio, and no neighbors for miles. I do not think anyone even knew anyone even lived there, and I wished I didn't!

I was bruised everywhere on my body, and I just wanted to die. I was getting close to having the baby and I just could not see why I needed to live except for bringing this baby into the world. I tried to cut my wrist several times but did not go deep enough to do damage. Once I closed myself up in the bathroom, but he broke down the door and beat me badly!

At some point my mom came to see me again to bring me some food while he was at work. Of course, she saw the bruises and I told her that I had fallen down the outside stairs, and hit my head on the ground, but she was not stupid! She went home and told dad that they needed to get me out of that 'hell hole' before he killed me. I was close to having the baby, so I stayed with my parents a little longer (without him knowing). I was preparing to leave him, but had he known, he would have killed me.

I went back after I had a baby boy, and for a few months there was 'love' in the house. Things changed for a while, but now he was jealous that the baby was getting more attention than he was getting. I remember taking the dirty laundry up the road about 6 miles to go to the laundry mat while he watched the baby.

I will never forget that day! When I got home with the laundry, I heard my two-month-old son screaming when I got out of the car. I ran in to see what was going on. He was 'black and blue' from being beat! I had only been gone for two hours!

I screamed, *"What happened?"*

And he said, *"He kept falling out of his crib."*

I knew better but confronting him would have cost us both our lives. He got so jealous when I picked up my baby, who was obviously in a lot of pain. Then he started in on me about how the baby was getting between us. So, now the truth comes out.

I could not call anyone, so I did not argue with him, or I would be next. The next day my mom came to see how I was doing. It was good timing because she saw what had happened to both of us. She realized that they needed to get me out of there fast, or we would both be dead.

They paid for the divorce and rescued us. I stayed with them, and they decided to send me to Fort Worth, Texas where a good friend was living, so I could go back to school and get my 3 credits to graduate high school. My mom took care of my baby boy while I was getting my credits. Unfortunately, my credits were not sent back in time for me to graduate with my class of 1969.

Thank God I was finally able to escape my nightmare on that street in the middle of nowhere!

Husband #2:

Oops! I Did It Again

(Technically Husband #1 Again)

So, about a year later, *David* and I ran into each other, and had a friendly conversation. This time it was different. We both had grown up somewhat, and talked for a few months. He told me how sorry he was about how he treated us. We were kids then and still kids– but the year-plus away from each other helped us to see things a little differently. He told me that he never stopped loving me and would never lay a hand on either of us again.

I started sneaking out of the house to see him because my parents would not tolerate this game again! Fasten your seatbelts! We got married again! Looking back, I was not being very smart, but I was back in the 'small' town I grew up in. I had gone nowhere in life but in circles. I knew I did not want to live in a small town forever.

Once again, I fell for the simple words, *"I love you."* He moved us to Oklahoma City, OK, which was about 250 miles north. He was working with other family members in finance. He bought a beautiful home for us. I too went to work as a hairstylist. It was all good until drugs entered the equation. It was now 1971.

There began many rumors of affairs he was having with many different women. I felt like a total fool…again! Then he started abusing me again. Once again I decided to escape while he was at work. Since I had the only car, and he rode with his brother, he never thought I would leave him again.

My dad also showed up, and he and I threw everything I wanted to take into his car and off we went back to Texas. Dad did not give me a big speech when we got home. He was glad that we were safe.

Long story short – they moved me to Dallas, TX, and I lived there for a year. Then I moved back to my small town in north Texas. From there I moved my son to southern Texas and started our lives all over again. I was free to move about. I never saw him ever again – ever! I cannot believe I made the same mistake twice, but God was faithful to get me out of there! I had learned my lesson, not once and for all, but twice and for all!

Husband #3:

Playing for the Other Team

After moving back to my hometown in north Texas again, I got a job working for a large company. I became an accountant's assistant for the office with about 15 other girls. While I was there, I met a computer programmer, who was about three years older than me, and he had worked for the same company for close to five years.

I met him because I was the person who took all the important paperwork to his office. We later dated for about six or seven months, and he asked me to marry him. Plus, he wanted to move to south Texas where he had gone to college at The University of Texas. I was all over moving to Austin. That was where I had taken my state board exam for cosmetology several years before. I always said I wanted to move there someday, so we moved!

We had only been there less than two years when he told me about a guy friend that he wanted to visit. When he got home, we had a talk about his visit. This time it was a strange but mutual decision to get a divorce.

I found out that he had a 'boyfriend' he lived with while in college. Apparently, he still had feelings for this friend in ways I was not used to, and I certainly was not going to be a part of any of it. So, I left him and filed for a divorce. I wish I had known before I married him that he was playing for the other team.

Husband #4:

Unfaithful

I loved Austin, Texas, so I got a job on The University of Texas campus cutting hair for a well know hair salon. We served both women and men who were mostly college students and businessmen. It was a beautiful place to live, and I loved it. Plus, I made pretty good money!

I worked there for close to 4 years tirelessly raising my son on my own. I had to work hard for the two of us, but it was worth it.

My boss, the owner of the salon on the University of Texas campus, had built a new salon on the 10th floor of the American Bank tower in downtown Austin. Let's call him *Dale*. So, *Dale* wanted to sell it because he just did not have the time to keep it up. He put it up for sale, and I overheard that he wanted $50,000 for it. Over the years I became business-smart in my own ways. I was a hardworking, single mom who had been messed over several times, but I was not stupid when it came to business matters.

So, I asked *Dale* if we could talk about the downtown salon. I told him that I was interested in purchasing it as is. I asked him what was the least he would sell it for?

He replied, *"$50,000"*

I replied, *"I'll give you $5,000, no more!"*

He laughed in my face, but I was serious! I told him that if he did not sell it to me, I would go to the IRS and let someone know that he has been paying all of the stylists, me included, with half cash and half check for the past four years to avoid paying as much in taxes.

I do not think you want to go to prison for a long time, I told him!

Bottom line, I bought the salon for $5,000 not $50.000. Three years later. I sold it for $21,000.00.

As the owner of a prestigious salon in downtown Austin, I met a guy one day at the local park, close to the salon I owned. I took my then six-year-old son to get some fresh air and walk through the park one beautiful sunny day. As we were just enjoying our time together, a nice guy, who was there walking his dog, struck up a conversation with me.

He told me he had gone to college in the south Texas area. I was familiar with where he mentioned. He also mentioned he had been married for 5 years, but his wife cheated on him too many times. He decided to move on with his life, was now divorced and looking to move to the Austin area and start a construction company.

We dated for several months. I met his family, and they liked me and my son. Soon we moved in together and started a relationship. What was important was that he was good to us. I took him back to meet my mom and dad. They liked him as well. We married and started a business together. Everything was great until…..I found out that he was having an affair on the side. He had two children with this woman while we were still married, and that is a game I do not play!

Our pastor at the time thought I should forgive him and work things out. I told the pastor that I can forgive, but working things out was not going to happen! I can do bad by myself, so I started all over again. This time I moved; I became a manager for a large craft franchise in south Texas. I just wanted to get as far away from Austin, Texas as I could get. So that was divorce #4. This was the husband that was unfaithful to me.

Husband #5:

Only On Paper

I lived in Killeen for close to 2 years. I loved being the manager of the largest craft store in Texas. While I was there, I got involved in a women's pool league, (as in shooting pool, not swimming) Our women's team won state, and we were headed to Las Vegas to play in the playoffs. It was awesome to have our team do so well, but we didn't win, so back home to Killeen, Texas, we flew.

I just could not get Austin, Texas out of my head. I knew my way around and I longed to be back in the city I loved.- Austin. It was like I needed to be there if I wanted to make a better life for my daughter. While in Killeen, I met a nice guy who just wanted to help me out. He got food for us at the PX on base and brought it over to us every Friday. I know this sounds crazy, but he told me that if we were married (*only on paper*), I would be able to go on base and get what I needed anytime. I could get food or gas anytime I needed

it. However, he needed to leave Texas and go back up north to take care of his mom. That was fine with me! I did not need another man in my life to hurt me again.

So, I married him *"on paper"* and took his last name. I never saw him again, and a few years later I filed for a *"paper"* divorce through an attorney in Austin so it would be on file. I was able to move forward with my life except for taking his name. I was stuck with it. My marriage to him was on paper and so was his name!

At the Well

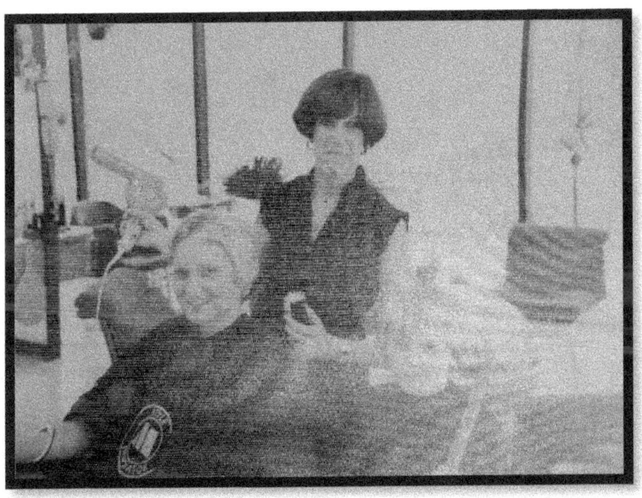

I am one of a few children who grew up in what I could call a *real home*. My parents did not fight. They did not drink or do drugs nor did any of us three children. My mother was a housewife while my dad worked to support a family of five. No one could have asked for better parents. I grew up thinking that life was supposed to just be like that. Married to one person, living in a nice house with a white picket fence with two or three children and no wants or needs. I thought my life was supposed to be *"perfect"* just like my parents.

Having given you some history, I want to fast-forward my life to the year 1975. By then I had married and divorced my first boyfriend, who was the father of my first child twice, along with three different other marriages. I was 24 years old and the owner of my own styling salon in a high-rise building downtown Austin, Texas. The new boyfriend and I were living together. Married life was for me, but not the guys I was choosing. You could say I was attracting the bad boys, but I was a nurturing soul, and I knew that I could fix them. Well, we all know how that ends.

By now I was into living life in the fast lane feeling like I was on one hand a loser and on the other hand, I was a successful business owner. I turned to drugs to ease the pain of living in both worlds. I just started snorting cocaine and speed to keep up with the fast-paced life I was living, and smoking dope to bring me down. Uppers during the day and downers in the evening or was it the other way around? After all, I owned my own business, and people could not tell that I was high most of the time. What was the harm?

At the salon, I had a shampoo lady working for me by the name of Wilma. One day she invited me to an outdoor revival that was going on at her small Black Baptist church just off east 16th St. She had noticed me, reading a pocket New Testament during some downtime in the salon. I do not know why I picked it up. I just got caught up in Jesus turning the water into wine, and so the word of God began to come alive in my soul.

I tried to share what I was reading with some of the girls that work for me. Each story jumped out of the page and into me, and I found myself wanting business to slow down just so I could read more.

My sister worked for me at the salon, and she did not understand why I would get so excited about how water turned into wine or how Jesus would just pass by a crowd and people were healed. Well, I did not understand either, but the stories kept pulling me in. I was not crazy, but I knew that something was going on.

By the time I went to the outdoor revival, my heart was ready. It did not take much for me to run to the altar when they gave the altar call. I brought my then boyfriend with me that night, and the same thing happened to him. We both gave our hearts to the Lord at the little Baptist church on E. 16th St. in a parking lot revival on a beautiful September evening in 1975. My soul was overwhelmed.

For the next three nights in a row, I found myself waking up, looking at the clock, getting up to get a glass of water, going to the restroom and then back to bed to get a few more hours of sleep. It was the second night that I realized I had woken up at the same time the night before 1:11am . The third night was the same at 1:11am, and by then I was feeling that someone or something was trying to get my attention, and the feeling was scary yet exciting.

Could this be God doing this? I remember going to work on the fourth morning and while I was in the middle of giving a haircut, God spoke to me, and I spoke to him while never missing a stroke of the scissors. It was like I was having an out of body experience. I was cutting hair, but I was planning on a date with God for that night at 1:11am again.

I was telling God that if it was really him to come back that night at the same time 1:11am. I was planning the robe I was going to wear after getting up out of bed and what would take place after that. It played out like a movie for what seemed to be several minutes. I envisioned exactly what I would do step-by-step after getting up out of bed. I wanted to prove this was all my imagination at the same time. It was like I was being lured in like a rabbit going into a cage to get the carrot.

My plan was to outwit God and stay awake until 1:11am came and went. Then I would not have known if it was really God. I guess you could say I was discerning before I knew what discerning was. I stayed awake up to what I remember as being really close to 1am. I do not ever remember when my head hit the pillow or when my eyes shut. All I know is that God put me to sleep, and God woke me up at 1:11am on the dot as though I had been asleep for hours.

My boyfriend had already gone to sleep. I did not tell him what was going on with me and my so-called date with God. He would have thought I was crazy and probably would have left me. I did not want to be alone again. Who in their right mind would believe? You are probably wondering yourself right now.

As my eyes opened, I looked over the clock and it said 1:11am. I knew right in that moment that I had to do just what I had told God I would do. Being a person of my word, God knew that I would follow through with what we had talked about earlier that day. I was about to meet the God of the universe face-to-face. Surely he would kill me and then no one would know what really happened to me because I had not told anyone about what was going on.

I got out of bed, went to my closet and in the dark I grabbed the robe I had envisioned I would wear. That scared me because my next step was to go to the front door and open it. I did not know what or who I was going to see on the other side of the door. I was so frightened, but I knew that there was no backing out now.

I reached for the doorknob and began to turn it slowly as I was shaking like I was sneaking up on God or something. I was shocked to see that no one was there, so I went outside and sat on the first of three steps that lead down to the parking lot of my fourplex. I looked around in the silence of the evening. There was not a cloud in the sky, and it was a beautiful September evening. I was not dead. I made it past opening the front door, so I thought that a good thing to do was pray, but I did not know how. I put my hands together like a child. That was a good place to start.

I remember my heart began talking to God with fear and excitement at the same time. I thanked him for not letting me die of heart failure by seeing him standing on the other side of the door when I opened it. All at once I heard noise like a mighty rush of wind coming from behind me through the trees. To say the least, I froze. I could not turn around and did not really want to. I knew that I was going to be like

Dorothy and the Wizard of Oz getting taken up and landing in another state by the force of the wind.

What I heard sounded like a tornado, but there was not a cloud in the sky. Where was this wind coming from? All I could do was hold my hands together even tighter as this wind blew right through me. I heard a voice in the wind that said peace be still.

Once again, I could not believe what I had just heard. I decided to go inside and open the Bible on my coffee table. Since I had never read the Bible, I had no idea what to read. I felt like I needed to read something. Then suddenly I remembered my mom telling me that when she was afraid, she would open her little 'pocket Bible and go straight to Psalms 23. She told me that it would comfort her and take away any fear.

So, I did the same thing. I picked up the Bible and it opened to the exact page of Psalms 23 without turning a page. I too felt the comfort my mom must have felt. I started reading the short scripture.

The open windows in the living room where I was sitting were just above my head. My windows were just above the parking lot wall, but there was no way to see into my apartment. It had to be at least eight feet down, so I felt safe sitting there.

As I began reading Psalms 23, I heard this horrible snarling and scratching on the window screen just above my head. I froze!

Suddenly I heard a voice saying, "Keep reading!" As I tried to focus on the scripture, a pillar of light stood just several feet in front of me, but I wasn't allowed to look straight at it. I did my best to finish the scripture. By then the snarling from the window stopped and the pillar of light left the room.

My eyes were glued to the verses of Psalms 23, and I continued to read. I know this all sounds weird, but everything has up until now. Trust me it was weird to me too!

Once again, I was in shock and could not believe what had just happened there. I was on the couch. I could not move so I just closed my eyes and I covered my face with my hands. As my hands were up I saw this heavy man's hand holding a hammer and anvil hitting on a rock. The hand hit the rock three times, and pulled back and as it did, I could see it was "JN IV" carved into the rock.

I opened my Bible to the front index to try to find what I saw, and that is how it was in the index. It was written just like I saw it when my hands were over my face. I knew I was being led to find it and read it. I looked at the page number and turned in the Bible to that page. Not really knowing why, I began reading. The story started off by talking about how Jesus and the twelve disciples were on a journey, and along the way, Jesus stopped at Jacob's well just outside Samaria. He told the disciples to go into the town and bring back some food. It was around high noon. As Jesus waited, there was a woman who came to draw water. So, Jesus asked the Samaritan woman if she would draw some water for him to drink.

"Therefore the Samaritan woman *said to Him, "How is it that You, being a Jew, ask me for a drink since I am a Samaritan woman?"

(For Jews have no dealings with Samaritans.)" **John 4:9**

*"He *said to her, "Go, call your husband and come here."* [17] *The woman answered and said, "I have no husband." Jesus *said to her, "You have correctly said, 'I have no husband';* [18] *for you have had five husbands, and the one whom you now have is not your husband; this you have said truly."* **John 4:16-18**

You'll need to read John, chapter 4 to see more of what her reaction was, but let me tell you what mine was..... It was right then that I realized this wasn't just a story. It was my story! It was ME that He was talking to. There was no where for me to run and hide. I had the same story. I was always looking for love in all the wrong places.

Jesus was showing me just like he did the woman at the well that if I continue to drink from the well of this world that I would never be satisfied. He was showing me that He was all I needed. You see I am the modern-day woman at the well. I had been married five times and was living with a man that very night God called me to Him when He woke me up at 1:11am four nights in a row. GOD told me I would never thirst again if I continued to drink His living water - His Word. I will never forget how He called me out - even while I was living in sin.

Give your life to the Lord and allow Him to do what He does best. He created each of us with a plan and purpose. We do not belong to ourselves. To let you know the scratches on the screen were real. The next morning there were deep clawlike tears on the screen just above where I sat on the couch.

My life has never been the same and it was not because I was scared into believing in God. He knew I was not happy with my life and that I needed something worth living for. I began to give God my all, and I put all my past failures under the blood of

Jesus. God forgave me and He became my everything.

After the Well

Many are called but a few are chosen, and I knew that he had chosen me to be a warrior for the kingdom of God. This was not a sweet little prayer to come to Jesus. This was a warfare that took place. I knew that there was not anyone like Jesus that would care about me as much as I needed to be loved and cared for. I made Jesus my husband, my best friend, my lover, my everything. Now I had a peace in my heart if I were to ever have my heart's desire, it would be on God's time and terms not mine.

Jesus was with me, even in my wrong decisions, and He was the only one who held my head up and moved me forward. God is a gentleman. He allows us to get past ourselves to the place of needing Him. And He is always there with open arms. Always!

There was a moment in time where I had enough. I took a trip to Daytona Beach, Florida to see a good friend who was a Christian. I had known her when I lived there years ago. After I had settled in at her home, I told her I would be right back. I went to the ocean just a block away from her house. I stood where the sky met the ocean and cried. I looked up, as though I was talking right to God and said,

"How dare you make me and not make someone for me! That has to be the cruelest joke you could have

ever played on me. What kind of God are you?"

I kicked sand in His face and walked away...

The Husband God Made for Me: *God Can Give You the Man of Your Dreams*

I have had several friends ask me to post how I met the man the Lord made just for me. Well, to begin you must ask God for him. It is really that easy, but the journey is tough. By that I mean, you need to do something. You need to stop trying to make it happen yourself. Your direction should be to get your life to the Lord and let Him do what He does best. You see, after five failed marriages, I finally got it!

For the next three months I did not date or go out to the clubs. I just stayed away from all temptations. I just wanted to stay focused on the Lord and the promises He had for me. I did not have to see to believe. I went back to the way I was when I first loved him.

This is when I had the church as my covering and when I spent time in the Word and in prayer. I knew that I had to prove to myself that if I want the blessings of God, I needed to let go of the ways of the world.

I do not mind giving you the good, bad, and ugly of my life because I have learned over the years that to be victorious over Satan, we must expose the enemy with everything that is within us. If you do not, you will never get victory! He is doing his job – so we need to stay ahead of the game and stop giving him things to use against us. It is okay if you must start over again. *"Never give up! Never surrender!"* That is what I would tell myself all the time.

Matthew 6:33 says, *"But seek first His Kingdom and His righteousness; and all these things will be added to you."*

It was 1991 and I had moved back to the Austin area after I had lived in Harker Hights, Texas, just North of Killeen where I was a store manager for Crafts Etc. After being married and divorced more times than

I would like to admit, I wanted to do something different. I was done with styling hair and being a manager/owner of a company.

I wanted to do something completely different. So, I picked up the newspaper, The Austin-American Statesman, and searched the 'job' section. I came across an ad that said, *'Private Investigator Needed.'* Why not see if I can qualify with all my cheating ex-husband experiences? Why not?

I called the private investigating agency and set up an appointment for an interview. We set a time to meet at a local café. She and I got along good. It was the best interview I had ever had! Of course, it started with a background check along with fingerprints. And of course I checked out. Within a week, I was a licensed private investigator for the state of Texas. It just does not get any better than that! My job was to go after the bad guys. I was assigned to drug, murder, and domestic cases. I was all in and I was good at it!

The owner of the agency had several sons. The next to the oldest was not the sharpest tool in the tool shed. He was someone that you just would not get advice from. However, one day he and I were talking and he said, *"Carol, you need to put an ad in the paper and find someone to date."*

I looked at him and said, *"You have got to be out of your mind! You do know what I do for a living, right"?*

He kept trying to convince me that since he had found a nice girl, I would find someone just as nice. He reassured me that it was very private, and no one would have my phone number.

After a few weeks of him telling me about this dating ad I gave in and told him that I would do it for just two days and that was it! So, I called the newspaper ad department and spoke with the person who took down the information. I cannot remember all the ad said, but I do remember that I said, *"law enforcement only need apply"* along with, *"Grace Slick look alike."*

It was unlike any of the ads other women were writing. *(You would have to be living in the 70's to know Grace Slick)*. I did not just want my ad to say, "36-24-36". I did not need or want those guys hitting on me!

Surprisingly, I had several messages on a recorded voice mail. I was in charge of calling the recorded message number that was given to me to check my messages. I liked the privacy factor. I had the choice to return the calls or not!

So, I listened to the voicemails and called back the first message. We met up to shoot pool. I beat him, and we never had a second date.

Benjamin, on the other hand was getting out of the army after several years in Germany and Iraq during Desert Storm (Desert Shield). It was his last week at Fort Hood, Texas before returning to his home state of New Mexico. He did not have much to do. He was just waiting for the paperwork, and that took several weeks. He did not have anything else to do, so he walked in the rain across the parking lot to pick up the Sunday paper.

When he went to reach for a paper there were none left – except for the one in the display window! So, he grabbed that one and headed back to the barrack to dry off. While reading the newspaper, he saw my ad in the dating section. He liked the idea that I was in law enforcement because he had also been a police officer back in New Mexico before going into the army. Plus, he liked the way I presented my ad. He called the voice mail number and left me the nicest message I have ever heard. My insight told me he was not a player. He was such a gentleman, and I could also tell he was very well educated. I called back the number he left. *(And yes, I called collect ladies!).*

So, for the next few hours I was busy chasing someone who needed to be caught, doing something they should not have been doing! Did I mention that I love my job? I was not thinking that Benjamin was waiting for me to call back right away. I just wanted to go home and relax with my daughter.

So, once I got settled in, I called Benjamin collect again. He said he was worried I would not call back. Remember we did not have cell phones back then, so everything was on the landline.

I told him I was sorry, but I was working. Our conversation went on for three plus hours *(on his dime)!* It had been hard for me to talk about me to someone I barely knew. But we talked about everything except sex or anything sexual. That would have changed the conversation, but it never went in that direction. That was refreshing for a change.

We both were looking for more than just another night out for dinner, a movie and sex for dessert. We talked about our goals, our dreams, and most of all, our relationship with God and what our beliefs were concerning Christianity. I certainly did not want to hook up with someone with different beliefs. So, after three hours on the phone, we decided to call it a night.

After hanging up the phone, I sat at my desk and thought to myself how nice this guy was, and he was so easy to talk to. My daughter walked into the room about the time I said to myself, *"Is this for real"?*

Soon after saying that, the phone rang. I answered it and the voice said, *"Is this for real?"*

It was Benjamin calling me back! Okay, just a little too freaky for me but it was cool to have that happen! That was when I said to him, *"I think we need to meet!"*

So, we planned for me to drive to Killeen the next evening to meet.

As I had mentioned earlier, I was a private investigator and the next morning I was on surveillance out in a small country town, by the name of Garfield, Texas. I was on the tail of an egg truck.

Surveillance consists of mostly waiting for the target of the investigation to show up. *"Hurry up and wait,"* was the game. Sometimes it was for hours and sometimes it was a quick catch for me. While just sitting and waiting for this egg truck to stop and deliver the store supplies along with drugs. Yes, I said drugs! I heard a voice say, *"This is going to be your husband for the rest of your life."*

I had never heard the voice of God, in my whole life, but I knew it was His voice! I grabbed my pad and pen and wrote down the exact words that I heard. When I looked up, there was the egg truck! I threw my writing pad into the back seat and now I was on duty to catch the bad guys.

After going in and doing my thing to get my information, I got in the car and went back to the office in Austin to report on the progress I had made in the case. However, the whole drive back, I could not get what just happened out of my head.

On the trip back, suddenly, I started thinking about the fact that I had no idea what this guy even looked like. Maybe he was ugly or really short, or he was a weirdo who stalked women. As fast as those thoughts came, they left.

Suddenly something happened in my heart. It did not matter about all the stuff that I thought mattered. For the first time in my life, it was not about the outside of someone and how they looked. This time it was about the inside of a person. Where was this coming from?

I drove to Killeen that night, which was about 40 minutes away. We met up on base at the location we agreed to at 6pm. We had decided to meet on a certain corner close to his dorm. I pulled up to the corner where he was standing. He got in my car, and I pulled into the parking lot a few yards away.

I still had not taken a good look at him, so I wanted to park the car, and get out. We both walked to the front of the car and hugged each other. I have never in my life felt what I felt in that hug. It felt like he went through me.

It was like electricity without shock. It was a feeling like no other. We became *"one in spirit"* in that moment. He felt it too. It was hard to let go of each other, but we did and then held hands and walked over to the picnic table and sat down.

I was 42 years old, and I felt like a schoolgirl on my very first date! As we sat and talked, he too expressed that he had never felt that electricity feeling as well. We talked and even kissed several times. We talked for quite a while and I told him that I needed to get back to Austin to pick up my daughter at her friend's house, plus, I needed to go to work in the morning.

He said, *"I don't want to lose you."*

I reassured him by telling him what happened to me that morning when I was on duty chasing an egg truck and the voice I heard. Then I went to my car and showed him the note that I wrote after hearing what I believed was the voice of God. I let him read for himself what God told me. Then we both cried. He looked at me and said, *"I have never told anyone this in my life, but I can honestly say that upon meeting anyone I dated, I never told them I love you and I don't want to lose you."* Of course, we both cried some more. This truly was a God thing that just happened.

What are the chances of two people, who never knew each other, to meet like this? I can tell you! I had asked God for a good man, and I was willing to give up my old ways to see what God had for me in my life.

This is not just another good story. This is what really happened. Once I had given myself and my heart completely to God, He gave me my heart's desire. Three days later I married Benjamin, the man God made for me.

Conclusion 

Whatever you are going through right now – separated, married, or divorced, know in your heart that God wants you to love Him more. He is a jealous GOD when it comes to our love for Him. That is what He is wanting for YOU as well. He is waiting for you to put HIM first in your life. As hard as that was to do, it is so worth the pay-off.

My life changed for the good when I gave my heart to the Lord, along with all the hurt and pain. If you can get glory out of what I have been through then use me. Lord God has put me a ministry for women that helps women to stop looking back in the rear-view mirror at the wrong choices they have made and begin to look at their future and to learn to walk in a love relationship with Jesus. The goal of this ministry is to enable them to be set free every time they share their story with someone else who has been beaten down by the storms of life.

Testimonies are given to the ones who can hold their heads up high and teach others from their experiences. I want my testimony to help women be delivered from Satan's lies that they are worthless and teach them to love Jesus more than anything or anyone. I know what a failure I felt like, and I almost did not make it through those years.

I can only imagine what the woman at the well felt like before Jesus passed by the well to speak to her. I know God wants all of us to use her and her pain to help others make it out and be set free. I know who I am in Christ, and I will continue to grow stronger every day until he calls me home. He helped me to know that Jesus already knew me even before I knew Him. He loved me just like I was.

Keep Him and He will give you your heart desires. Most of all never stop having a personal relationship with Jesus even when he does give you your heart's desire.

To God be the glory forever and ever! I have been married to the man God made for me, my husband for this lifetime for going on 31 years now. I am still going into the cities telling all those who will listen to me about a man who told me all the things that I ever did. Find my story in JN IV. I am the real-life woman at the well.

A Word from the Author

My prayer for you is for you to ask the 'Holy Spirit' to go before you in everything you face in life. I learned the hard way, but I learned to trust the Lord. *"Letting go and letting God"* was the answer. I pray every person who reads this book will become an OVER-COMMER I went from the lowest I have ever been - to becoming a Minister for the Lord.

Contact Information:

Carol Davis – Doswell

Minister Of Mentoring

☎ (816) 824-1201

✉ Colour.my.world777@gmail.com

Minister.of.mentoring111@gmail.com